Christmas Me[mories]

MELODY BOBER

8 Intermediate Piano Arrangements of the Season's Most Nostalgic Carols

The Christmas season brings a flood of wonderful memories from my childhood: trips to my grandparent's farm where the 15-foot tree was ablaze with light; the continuous buffet of homemade holiday treats; and the fellowship of aunts, uncles and cousins. These things truly made the holiday one of love and happiness.

Christmas morning was always exciting with the opening of gifts and discovering the treasures from Santa in our stockings. The day was complete with the reading of the Christmas story from Luke, Chapter 2 and the singing of traditional Christmas carols.

In *Christmas Memories, Book 2,* I share arrangements of some of my favorite carols. It is my hope that you enjoy practicing and performing the arrangements in this collection and that they will stir your hearts and re-kindle your own precious memories of this blessed season.

Merry Christmas!

Alfred Music

ISBN10: 0-7390-4915-1
ISBN13: 978-0-7390-4915-1

The First Noel

English Carol
Arr. by Melody Bober

Good Christian Men, Rejoice

Traditional German Carol
Arr. by Melody Bober

___∧_ simile_

Away in a Manger

Traditional
Arr. by Melody Bober

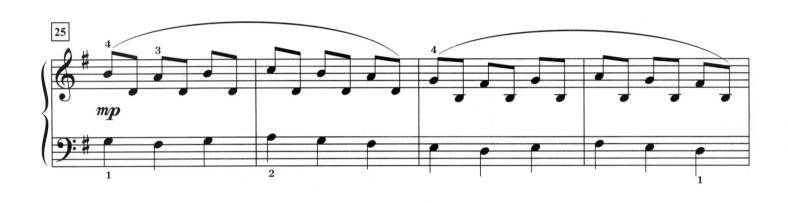

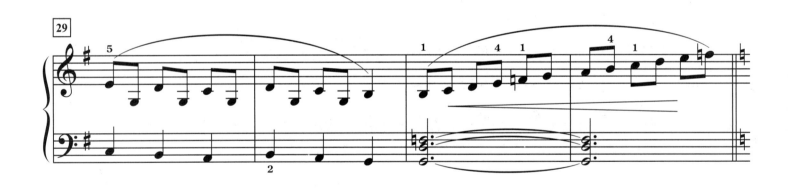

Reflectively ($\quarternote$ = 96)

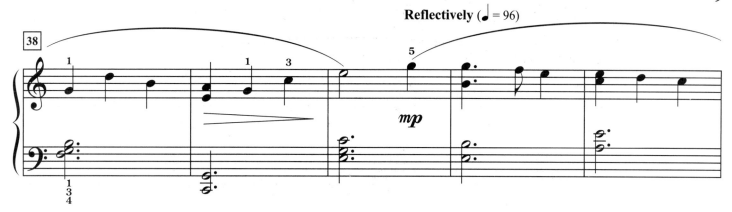

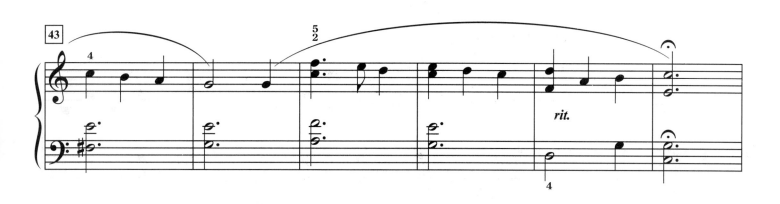

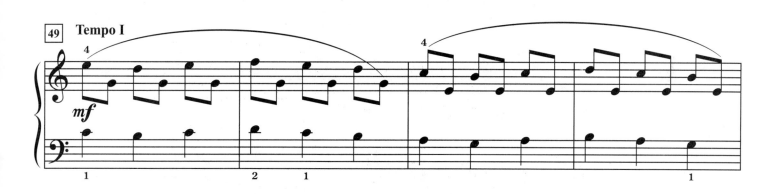

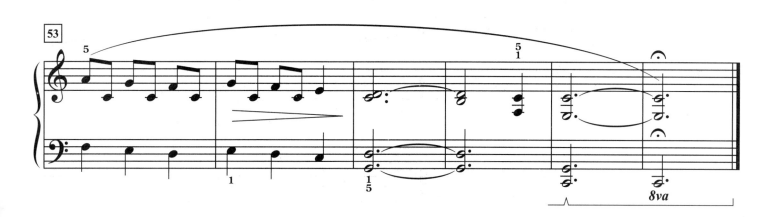

O Come, All Ye Faithful

J. F. Wade
Arr. by Melody Bober

With vitality and boldness ($\quad$ = 116)

Silent Night

Franz Grüber
Arr. by Melody Bober

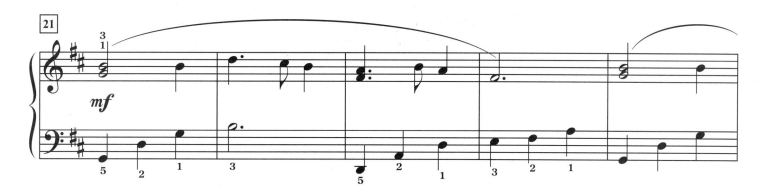

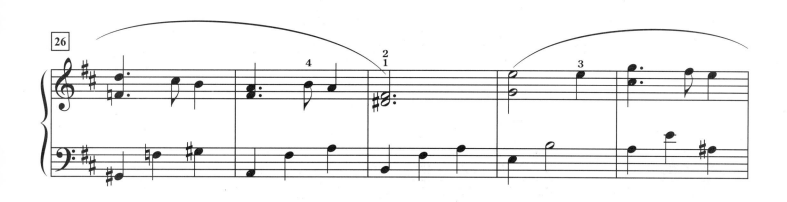

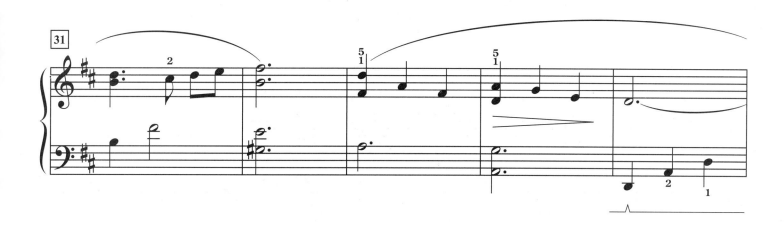

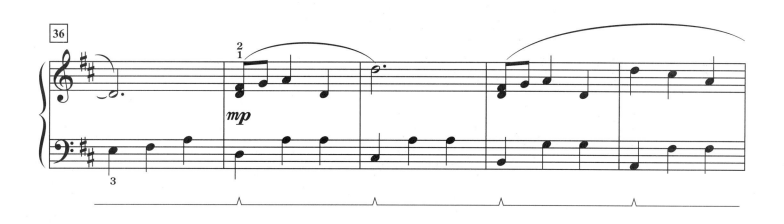

Angels We Have Heard on High

English Carol
Arr. by Melody Bober

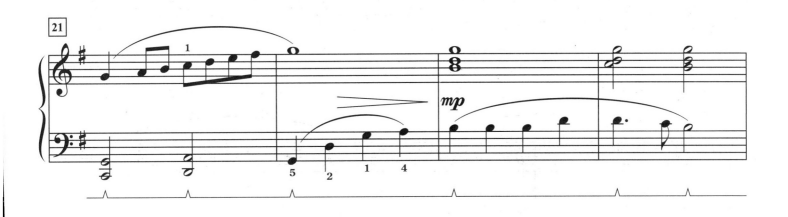

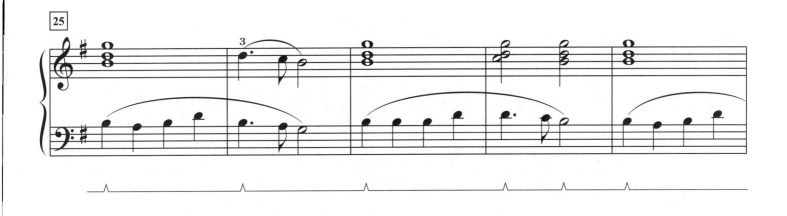

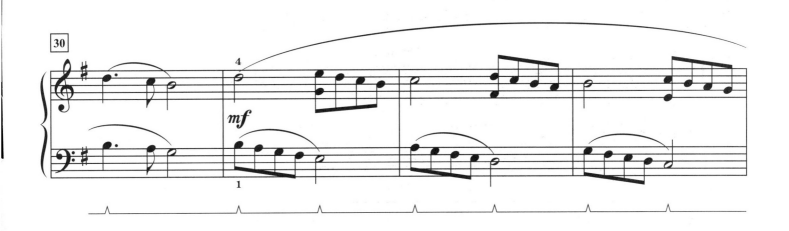

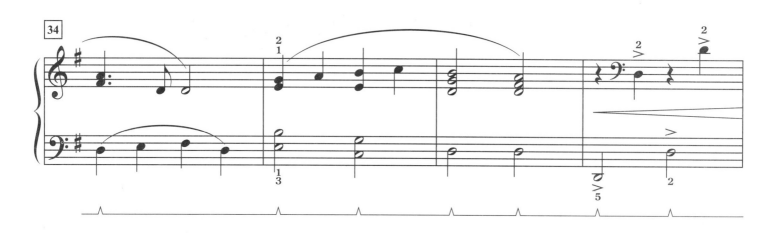

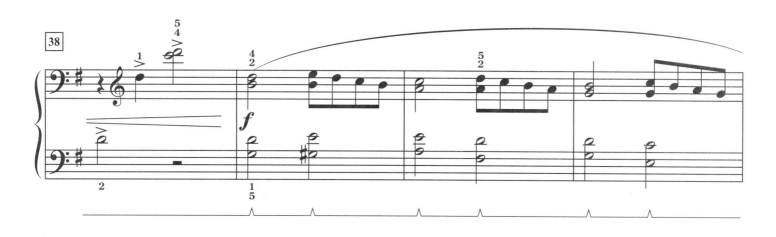

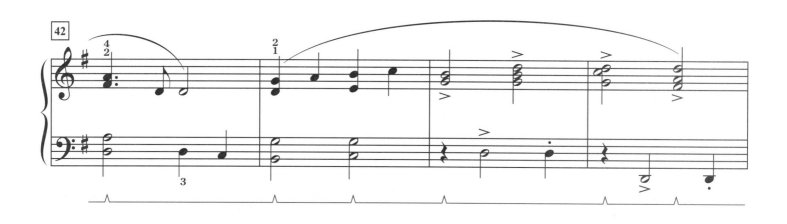

It Came Upon the Midnight Clear

Richard S. Willis
Arr. by Melody Bober

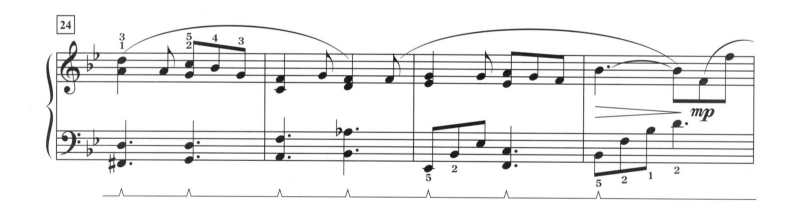

I Saw Three Ships

Traditional English Carol
Arr. by Melody Bober

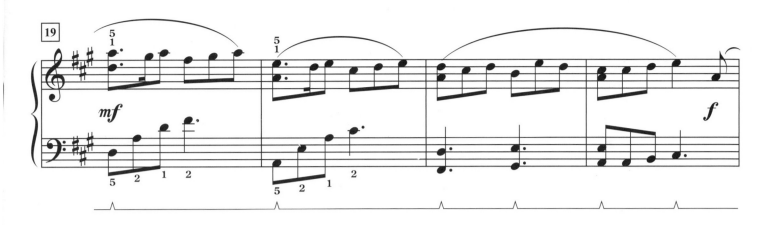

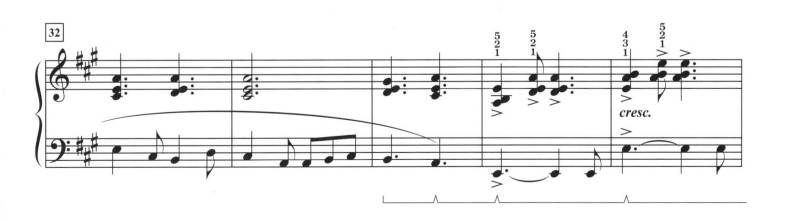